HAL•LEONARD
INSTRUMENTAL
PLAY-ALONG

AUDIO ACCESS
INCLUDED

VIOLIN

Piazzolla Tangos

T0070474

To access audio visit:
www.halleonard.com/mylibrary

Enter Code
4284-0981-4948-2249

ISBN 978-1-4950-2843-4

BOOSEY & HAWKES

AN IMAGEM COMPANY

DISTRIBUTED BY

HAL•LEONARD®
CORPORATION
7777 W. BLUEMOUND RD. P.O. BOX 13819 MILWAUKEE, WI 53213

www.boosey.com
www.halleonard.com

AUSENCIAS
(The Absent)

VIOLIN

ASTOR PIAZZOLLA

EL VIAJE
(The Voyage)

VIOLIN

ASTOR PIAZZOLLA

CHANSON DE LA NAISSANCE
(Song of the Birth)
from FAMILLE D'ARTISTES

VIOLIN

ASTOR PIAZZOLLA

MILONGA
from A MIDSUMMER NIGHT'S DREAM

VIOLIN

Astor Piazzolla

LIBERTANGO

VIOLIN

ASTOR PIAZZOLLA

D.S. al Coda

CODA

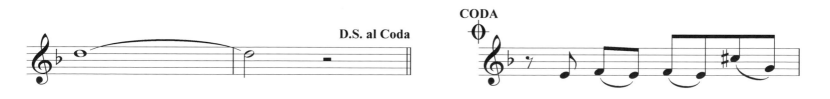

LOS SUEÑOS
(Dreams)
from SUR

VIOLIN

ASTOR PIAZZOLLA

OBLIVION

ASTOR PIAZZOLLA

VIOLIN

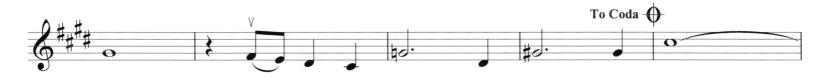

OUVERTURE
from FAMILLE D'ARTISTES

ASTOR PIAZZOLLA

VIOLIN

SENSUEL
(Sensual)
from A MIDSUMMER NIGHT'S DREAM

VIOLIN

ASTOR PIAZZOLLA

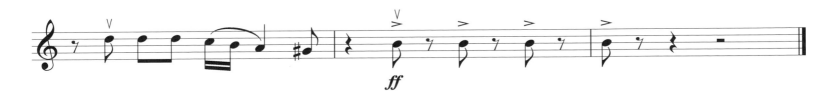

SENTIMENTAL
from FAMILLE D'ARTISTES

VIOLIN

ASTOR PIAZZOLLA

Moderate Tango

VUELVO AL SUR
(I'm Returning South)

VIOLIN

ASTOR PIAZZOLLA

SIN RUMBO
(Aimless)

VIOLIN

ASTOR PIAZZOLLA

STREET TANGO

VIOLIN

ASTOR PIAZZOLLA

TANGO FINAL
from FAMILLE D'ARTISTES

VIOLIN

ASTOR PIAZZOLLA